THE QWERTY MAD

#71

A Time Warner Company

WARNER BOOKS EDITION

Copyright © 1976, 1977, 1978 and 1986 by E.C. Publications Inc.
All rights reserved.
No part of this book may be reproduced without permission.
For information address:
E.C. Publications, Inc.
485 Madison Avenue
New York, N.Y. 10022

Title "MAD" used with permission of its owner,
E.C. Publications, Inc.

This Warner Books Edition is published by
arrangement with E.C. Publications, Inc.

Warner Books, Inc.
666 Fifth Avenue
New York, N.Y. 10103

 A Time Warner Company

Printed in the United States of America

First Printing: February, 1986

Reissued: July, 1991

10 9 8 7 6 5 4 3 2

ATTENTION SCHOOLS

WARNER books are available at quantity discounts with bulk purchase for educational use. For information, please write to: SPECIAL SALES DEPARTMENT, WARNER BOOKS, 666 FIFTH AVENUE, NEW YORK, NY 10103.

COUNTER-SCHLOCKWISE DEPT.

A few years ago, there was an Academy Award-winning movie about a woman whose husband was killed in an accident, leaving her with no money and a 12-year-old son to raise. Then some bright TV Network executive thought this would make a great premise for a weekly comedy series. The result? Well, all we can say is:

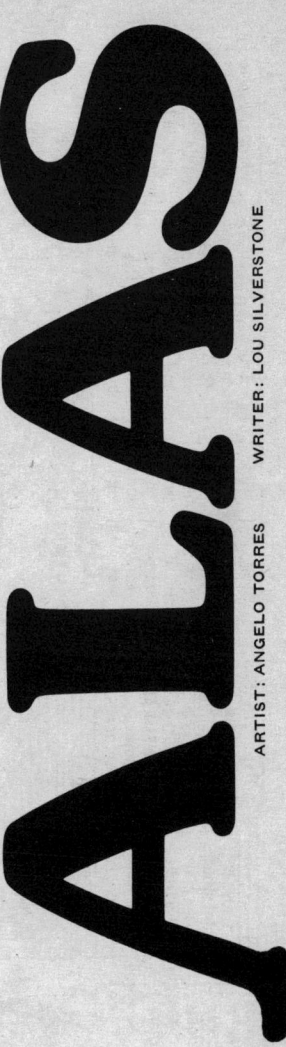

ARTIST: ANGELO TORRES WRITER: LOU SILVERSTONE

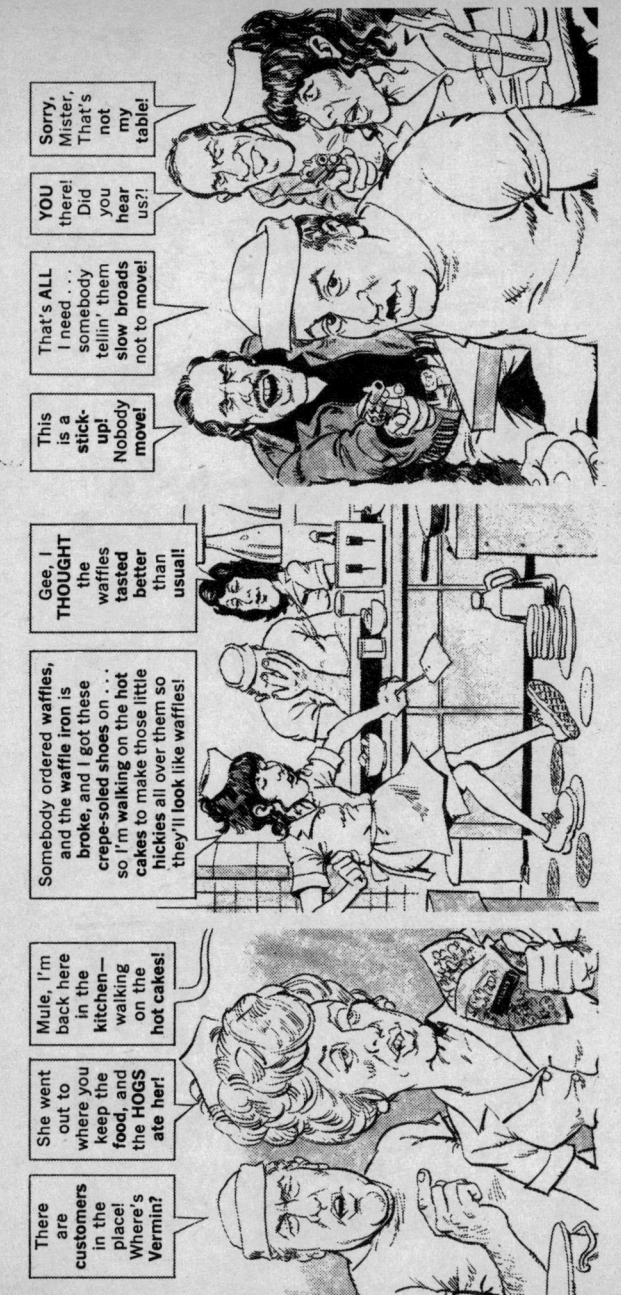

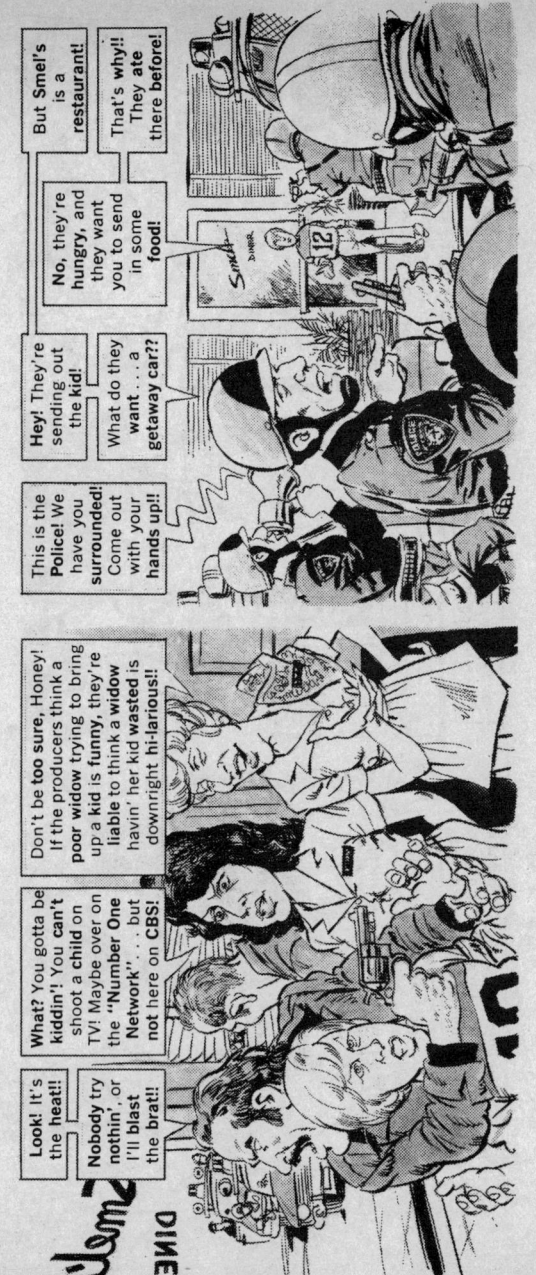

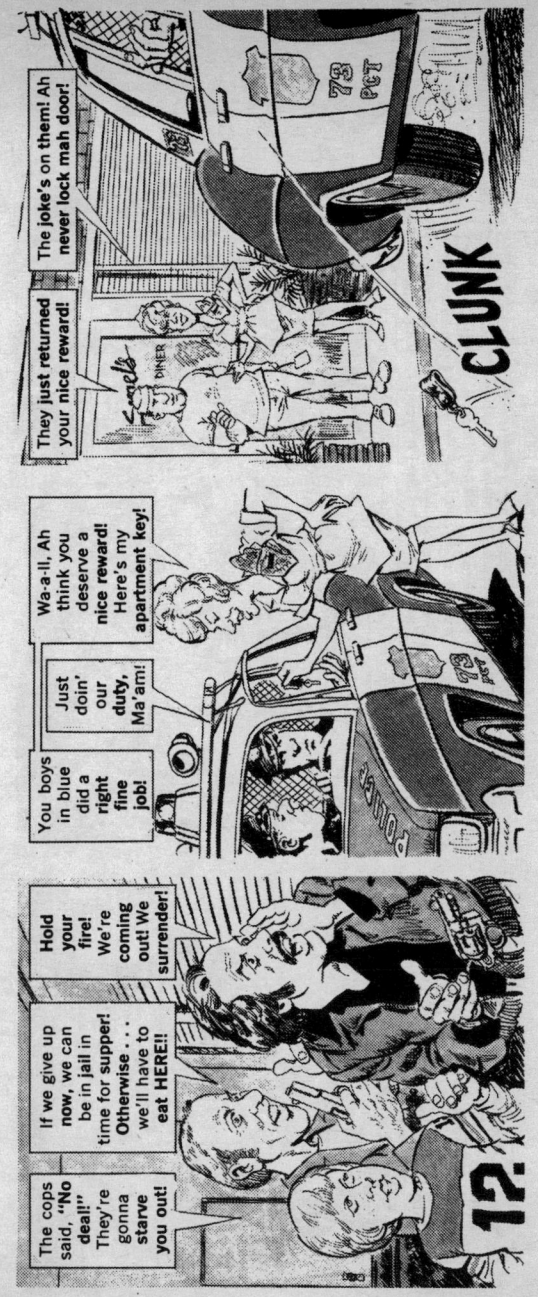

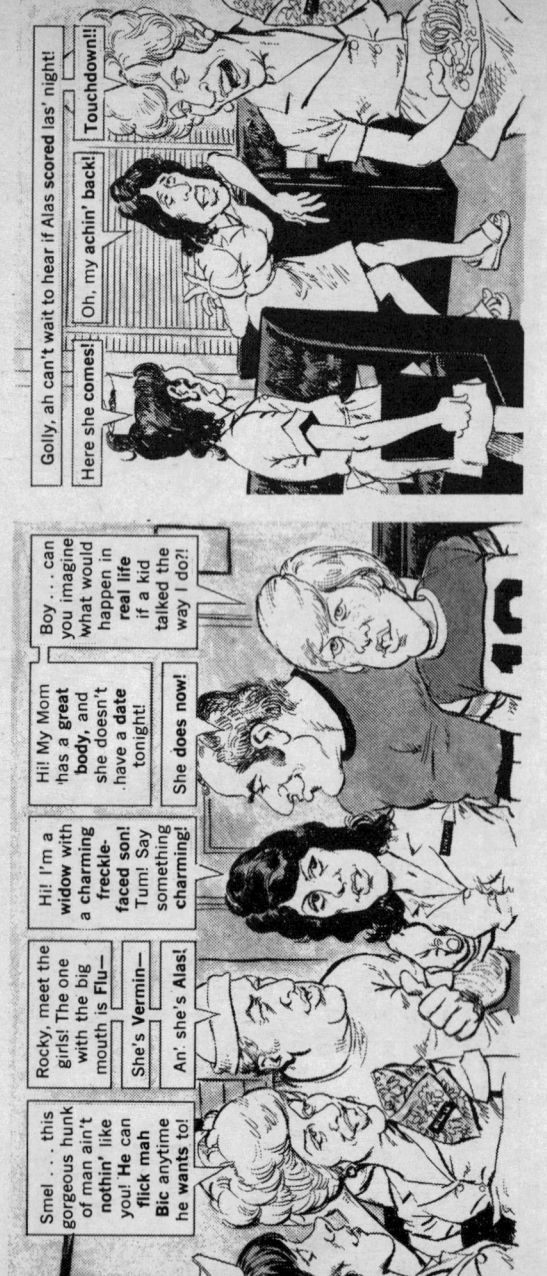

DON MARTIN DEPT.

LATE ONE AFTERNOON IN SOUTH DAKOTA

BERG'S-EYE VIEW DEPT.

THE LIGHTER SIDE OF...

FADS FADS FADS

ARTIST & WRITER:
DAVID BERG

SWITCH PITCH DEPT.

There are two things wrong with TV Commercials. They're stupid... and they're boring. The stupid part we can't do anything about because they're created by stupid people. The boring part is easy to fix. TV Commercials are boring because they're so utterly predictable. After watching for a few seconds, we know exactly what each one is going to say when it finally gets to the point. MAD, however, feels that TV Commercials really do not have to be dull and boring. Advertisers might do well to have us guessing rather than to have us asleep. And they can do that with

SURPRISE TELEVISION COMMERCIALS

ARTIST: JACK DAVIS   WRITER: TOM KOCH   IDEA BY: DEZI SZONNTAGH

JOKE AND DAGGER DEPT.

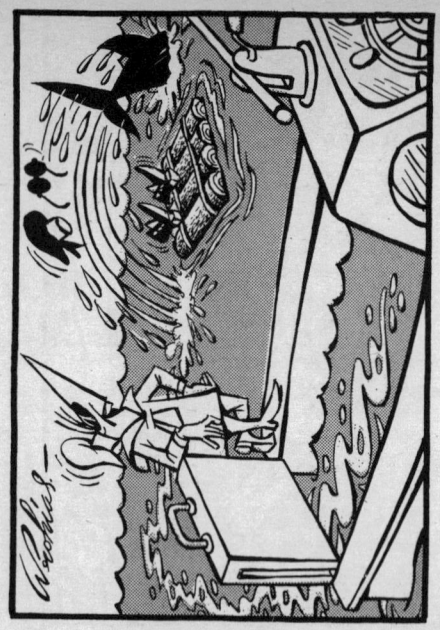

SHTICKS ON STONES DEPT.

Cemeteries are real downers, and they certainly aren't "fun" places to visit. But they *could* be if their tombstones and grave markers were jazzed up with inscriptions that told about the poor departed people beneath them in cute, light, clever, humorous ways. Mainly, we'd like to see something like these

DISTINCTIVE
MAD EPITAPHS

ARTIST: BOB CLARKE   WRITER: FRANK JACOBS

FOR A TIGHTROPE WALKER

ORRIN SMEED
1916-1966
USED NO NET
SHOWED NO FEAR
MADE MISSTEP;
WOUND UP HERE.

FOR A SWIMMER

LANCE LINGUINI
1950-1975
SAW FIVE SHARKS
OFF THE COAST.
FOUR HE MISSED—
ONE ALMOST.

FOR A NOVICE FARMER

BEN ESTERHAZY
1939-1975
HERE LIES BEN,
WHOSE LIFE WAS FULL—
TILL HE TRIED
TO MILK A BULL.

FOR AN URBAN DWELLER

RALPH
DINWIDDIE
1915-1971
RALPH FOUND OUT
SURE AS HECK
MUGGERS WON'T
TAKE YOUR CHECK.

FOR AN OUTDOORSMAN

BRICE
FOLLABEE
1932-1969
IT'S TOO LATE
TO TELL YOUNG BRICE
SOMETIMES LIGHTNING
DOES STRIKE TWICE.

FOR AN AFRICAN EXPLORER

ZOLTAN
ZANDAR
1911-1968
ZOLTAN LEARNED
WITH REGRETS
RHINOS DON'T
MAKE GOOD PETS.

FOR A PRINTER

MORRIS
MEERSHAUM
1920-1961

STOOD TOO CLOSE
TO THE PRESS;
NOW THIS IS
HIS ADDRESS.

FOR A VICTIM OF THE MOB

EDWARD
STARKRAVING
1933-1969

EDWARD LEARNED
WITH DISMAY
LOANSHARKS MEAN
WHAT THEY SAY.

FOR A HEART ATTACK VICTIM

DWIGHT
FLENSCH
1903-1970

DWIGHT PULLED THROUGH
WITH GREAT WILL;
THEN, ALAS,
CAME THE BILL.

FOR A SKY DIVER

KNUTE
KNOPP
1935-1976
IN MID-AIR,
LUCKLESS KNUTE
LEARNED THAT MOTHS
ATE HIS CHUTE

FOR A DOG FANCIER

DUDLEY
GROON
1904-1973
NO ONE TOLD
POOR OLD DUDLEY
DOBERMANS
JUST AREN'T CUDDLY.

FOR A MOTORIST

GLENN
SCHNURR
1937-1975
TRIED TO PASS
TRAILER TRUCK;
FOUND OUT QUICK
WHAT'S A SCHMUCK.

TRIPPING WITH THE LIGHTS IS FANTASTIC DEPT.

ARTIST: HARRY NORTH, ESQ.
WRITER: DICK DE BARTOLO

GOING OVER BARD DEPT.

A MAD TREASURY OF *Shakespeare's Lesser Known Quotations*

ARTIST: HARRY NORTH, ESQ.
WRITER: DENNIS SNEE

If something is rotten in Denmark, then haste; get thee to Sweden.

* * *

Talk and talk and talk. Were it not for ears, who would know?

* * *

Judge not Leonard by the length of his beard, nor its color, but by the number of crumbs therein.

* * *

Lo, in Heaven there sits a judge no king can corrupt. Nor will he lend money, save to certain close friends.

* * *

Better a solitary man than relatives in the bathroom.

* * *

A tragic tale is best for winter. In summer, 'tis off to the beach.

Could Richard stop death? Could Henry? If they were here, you could ask them.

* * *

Of valor, discretion is the better part; of dinner, dessert.

* * *

O! The dawn! Would it only come back in half an hour!

If your boots are heavy, take them off. But pray, not here.

* * *

You speak of that adultress as if she were a rose, and you but a pound of fertilizer.

* * *

Yea, his evil may live after him, but his best suit he takes to the grave.

* * *

Her tears, Polonius, are as false as thy teeth.

* * *

Youth, in froth and frolic, play. But when age doth come, no elder catches the speedy young tart.

* * *

Sad, sad, and sad again. His love is gone, but his wife remains.

* * *

In the sight of men, take only your due. But when alone, grabbeth what you can.

* * *

Gladly I would drink the hemlock, my son, but then who would wash the cup? Not you, for sure. The state of thy room announces your talents.

Women, Mercutio, are the itch we gladly scratch.

* * *

In such a night did Orestes take flight, and tripping on a pail, did break his ass.

* * *

Trust not the woman, Horatio, who kisses her husband, then wipes her lips.

* * *

Doth yonder fat man think himself thin? Bring him, then, thy mirror, and none of my mutton.

DON MARTIN DEPT.

ONE EVENING IN A HOLLYWOOD TV STUDIO

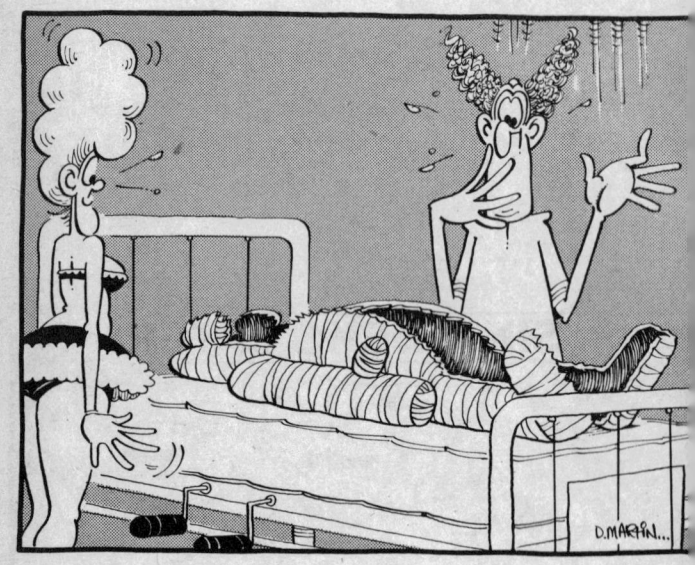

CREATURE PRESENTATION DEPT.

Monsters and unknown creatures such as "Big Foot", "The Abominable Snowman", "The Loch Ness Monster", etc., have always fascinated people. Zoologists, biologists, scientists and just plain monster freaks have been searching for these creatures for years. And so far, they haven't found a single one. They haven't even found any proof that they exist. But they keep looking, and they keep making movies and TV shows about them. Which got us to wondering: How do you make a documentary movie about something that doesn't exist? And why bother? Well, we got the answer to 'Why bother?' ("Monster movies make a lot of bread, man!") when we asked Mr. Sidney Splicer, a successful documentary film-maker, who invited us to a screening of his latest "In Search Of...", flick. So join us now as...

MAD GOES TO A PREVIEW OF AN "IN SEARCH OF..." MOVIE

ARTIST: JACK DAVIS   WRITER: LOU SILVERSTONE

SPLICER FILMS
PRESENTS
IN SEARCH OF BIG TUSH

From this title, you probably think we found a brand new monster, right? **Wrong!** That's what we *think*! Actually, we DON'T want you to think! Actually, we DON'T say that we FOUND "Big Tush"! We only say that we're SEARCHING for "Big Tush"!

In order to make an "**In Search Of . . .**" movie, you gotta have something to **Search** for! And all the old reliables . . . like "**Big Foot**" and "**The Loch Ness Monster**" and "**Noah's Ark**" have been done! So we had to discover a new one!

And how do you discover a new monster? Simple! You make one up!

Then, all you need are plenty of film clips, a large tube of splicing glue . . . and you're in the film-making business!

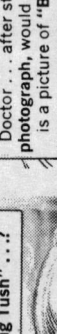

 Notice how cleverly we led into "The Loch Ness Monster"? What does "The Loch Ness Monster" have to do with "Big Tush"? Nothing! But every film clip library has tons of film on Loch Ness, and no "In Search Of . . ." monster movie is complete without some mention of old "Nessie"!

Behind me is the dark, murky waters of **Loch Ness**, home of the legendary "**Loch Ness Monster**"! There have been hundreds of sightings of this creature since it was first seen by St. Columba in 565! Is "The Loch Ness Monster" **fact** or **fiction**?

St. Columba said "**fact**"!

And after all, would a Saint LIE?!

While we are at the film library, we **also** got a few clips of the "**Easter Island Statues**," which have even **less** to do with "**Big Tush**" than "**The Loch Ness Monster**"! But, believe me, it isn't easy stretching a movie like this to 90 minutes!

There are many mysteries that have baffled science, like the famous "**Easter Island Statues**"! Doctor Cranium, how did these sixty-ton, thirty-foot heads get here! And what do they mean . . .?

One theory is that they were from **outer space**! Notice how they seem to be wearing helmets!

Yes, but **WHY** were they brought here?

To get **RID** of them! Would **YOU** want one on your front lawn?!?

Old newspaper stories are another time-filling gimmick that helps provide the phony evidence that our creature really exists! I had these printed in an amusement park that has a place that does funny headlines for a buck!

There are written accounts of "Big Tush" sightings dating as far back as 1803, when Chinese railroad workers saw a creature that could have been "Big Tush"! Unfortunately, they could only speak Chinese, so there was no accurate description!

The most recent sighting was in the State of Washington by a couple of campers, Billy Joe and Mary Lou Backpacker...

The people who see these creatures are the same type of idiots who take the **Pepsi Taste Test**, or stop using **bleach** for a month, or appear on **quiz shows**! They sound so **ridiculous**, you **believe** them!

I—I seen him standing right over there, by that big tree!

And what was he doing...?

He was making a sissee!

He was goin' to the John!!

A.... WHAT?!?

Now, we bring back the "house scientist" to verify that this is a motion picture of "Big Tush". Actually, he doesn't verify it, but he gives a pretty definite "maybe"! Which is about all you ever get from one of these "In Search Of..." movies!

Doctor, have you looked at the Gwirtzman film?

Yes... and I've got the headache to prove it!!!

Is the thing in the film "Big Tush"— or is it a wild animal! Say, a bear?

No, the texture of the fur is too fine to be a bear! It more closely resembles RACCOON fur!!

Are you saying it's a raccoon?

Don't be silly! Who ever heard of an eight-foot raccoon?!

Notice how we cut the professor off in mid-sentence! He was about to say it could have been a college kid in a raccoon coat! That's what's known as "expert film sound editing"!

If it WASN'T a bear, and it WASN'T a raccoon... could it have been "Big Tush"...?

Well, yes, but—

DON MARTIN DEPT.
ONE MORNING IN A COURTROOM

THAT'S SHOE BIZ DEPT.

FOOTNOTES* TO LITERATURE

ARTIST: PAUL COKER, JR.   WRITER: PAUL PETER PORGES

*"So THAT's how you keep your men so merry, Robin!"

*"Number Eleven...! Thou shalt not throw temper tantrums!"

*"Hey! One for all . . . remember!?"

*"Alexander Portnoy! We're still waiting! What are you DOING in there?"

*"It may be agile, but it certainly isn't ARTFUL dodging!"

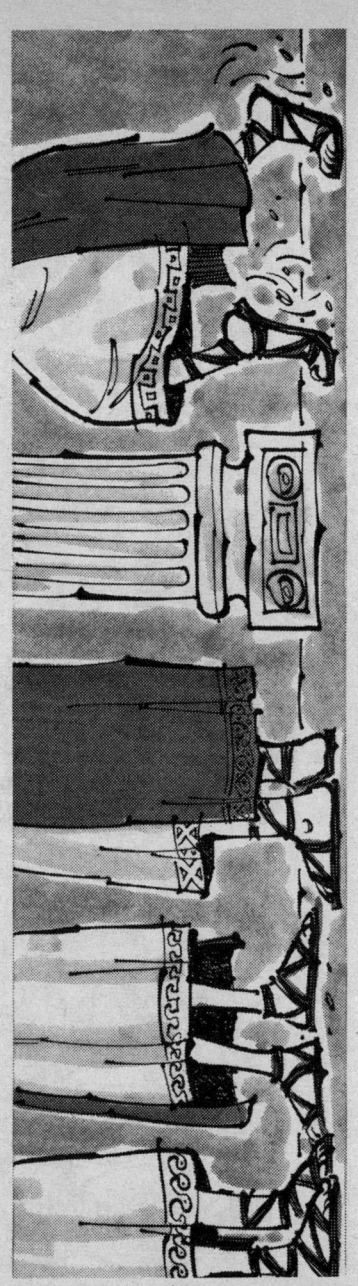

*"Where's Brutus...?"

*"Damn you, Moby Dick! Damn you, knotty pine!"

*"Don Corleone sends his compliments and says you don' owe him no more favors!"

FROM FAD TO VERSE DEPT.

THE RIME OF THE SKATE

(With apologies to Samuel Taylor Coleridg

He was a wild-eyed skateboard freak; "I've slalomed all through hell," he
He stoppeth one of three. "That's where I skinned my knee."

MODERN BOARDER

("Rime of the Ancient Mariner")

Written by Tom Koch   Illustrated by Don Martin

freestyled up the wall and back; He launched into his ghastly tale,
Then, crouching on his board,   While those around him snored.

"It started at a Skatepark near
My California home.
'Twas there I met two kindred souls,
Big Stan and Small Jerome.

"The three of us all shared the drea[m]
Of learning far-out tricks
Like tail-taps and three-sixty turns
To help us score with chicks.

Six days a week we practiced on
the Skatepark's asphalt deck.
(The seventh day, I washed my hair
and cashed my welfare check.)

"In time, we three had learned to do
The One-Wheel Pirouette;
And then we stopped to marvel that
No girls had noticed yet.

"Said Stan, 'I fear these hot-dog tricks
Will never land a dame.
So why not try for second best:
The Skateboard Hall of Fame?'

"The Hall of Fame!!?? We'd seen its plaques
And knew its honored types
Were those who'd dared to skate inside
Of giant, hollow pipes.

"Two stories high, those lengths of pipe
Loom o'er the desert floor,
Abandoned there by thirst-crazed men
Who'd passed that way before.

"To reach them, you must slog through sand
A hundred miles from town.
Still worse, when skating in a pipe,
You're often upside down.

"This prospect panicked Small Jerome,
Who asked, 'Why must we dare
To skate someplace we might get killed?'
Quoth Stan: 'Because it's there!'

"Such logic could not be denied
It drove us forth to meet
The destiny that lurked there in
The hellish desert heat.

"To make our trip a sure success,
We packed our kits with care.
I brought the jelly sandwiches,
The plates and silverware.

"Stan brought some skateboard urethane
In case the wheels got hot.
Jerome said he'd bring water bags,
But somehow, he forgot.

"And so, our throats became more parched
With every passing day.
Worse yet, we found no pipes to skate.
We'd clearly lost our way.

"As time slipped by, our hopes grew dim
Of ever being found.
Then, suddenly, a gopher popped
Its head above the ground.

"'A good luck omen!' cried Big Stan,
And Small Jerome agreed:
'A gopher-powered skateboard is
The very thing we need.'

"A tiny treadmill soon was built
Where gopher paws could run.
We nailed it to our strongest board;
Then climbed on, one by one.

"Big Stan yelled, 'Mush!' The gopher strained.
I felt the skateboard start!
And as it moved, a giant weight
Was lifted from my heart.

"We all felt cheered, and foolishly
We laughed and joked and talked;
For we had yet to learn how slow
A weary gopher walked.

"His treadmill pace was soon a stroll;
Our motion all but ceased.
Half crazed, I screamed, 'You goldbrick, you!'
And then I killed the beast.

"'You fink! You've killed our good luck charm!'
I heard Big Stan emote,
While Small Jerome the gopher tied
Around my pulsing throat.

"My former friends then left me there.
Stan put their reason well:
'In summer weather such as this,
Dead gophers tend to smell.'

"Left with the skateboard all alone,
Time weighed upon my hands.
It's hard to practice wheelies 'mid
The shifting, whisp'ring sands.

"In that unceasing desert heat,
My mind began to fail.
One time, I even thought I saw
The gopher wag its tail.

"Thus, I assumed my eyes played tricks
When on the seventh day,
A grizzled skateboard spook appeared,
And slalomed straight my way.

"I sensed he was no earthly thing,
For though his speed was great,
I saw his board had rusty wheels
From some old roller skate.

"His eyes were wild; his socks were torn;
His beard was long and fine.
Said he, 'That gopher 'round your neck
Was once a friend of mine.'

"'You killed my pal!' he shrieked at me.
'For that, you'll dearly pay.
My ghostly curse will follow you
Until it's Judgement Day.'

"He vanished, and I glumly thought
That things could not be worse.
Forever seemed like quite a while
To stay beneath a curse.

"I can't recall how long I'd walked
In mindless exercise
When far away, I thought I saw
A town of goodly size.

"It's only a mirage, I guessed.
No town could really be
In such a God forsaken spot.
Still, why not check and see?

"To my surprise, the town was real.
I whooped with sheer delight
To see old broads in tennis shoes
Stand bathed in neon light.

"'I'm saved!' I screamed at one old dame.
'This place is Xanadu!'
Said she: 'Las Vegas is its name,
I'll bet you five-to-two.'

"The gopher I soon flung aside
To toast my change of fate.
Its body struck a roulette wheel,
And stopped on number eight.

"'You win!' I heard a voice call out.
'That's quite a clever play.'
And then I saw the man in charge
Push piles of chips my way.

"I won a million bucks that night,
And made a gambler's vow
To have the custom skateboard built
That stands before you now.

"It's wheels are made of diamond dust
Mixed in with urethane.
The trucks are cast of solid gold.
The kicktail's teakwood grain."

The skateboard freak then paused amid
The tale he'd come to tell;
And as he hugged his costly board,
One teardrop on it fell.

Spake he at last: "I still have times
When sorrow seizes me.
A guy gets glum to know he's cursed
For all eternity.

"For though I've lived through my ordeal,
And ditched the gopher, too,
And have the finest skateboard known,
One thing still makes me blue.

"I'm doomed through life to tell my tale,
So ghastly and unreal.
If you've been bored to hear it once,
Just think how I must feel."

SECONDING OUR NOTION DEPT.

PRESENTING MORE ORIGINAL MAD COVERS 👉

AND ONE MAD MOMENT LATER! 👉

THE ORIGINAL

COVER...

...AND ONE

MOMENT LATER!

THE ORIGINAL

COVER...

...AND ONE

ARTIST: JACK RICKARD   WRITER: DON EDWING

MOMENT LATER!

THE ORIGINAL

COVER...

...AND ONE

MOMENT LATER!

THE ORIGINAL

COVER...

...AND ONE

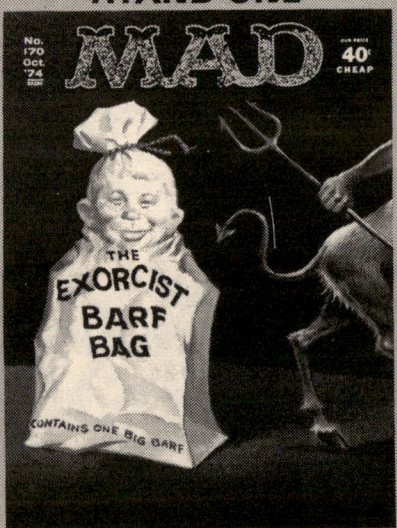

MOMENT LATER!

THE ORIGINAL

COVER...

...AND THREE

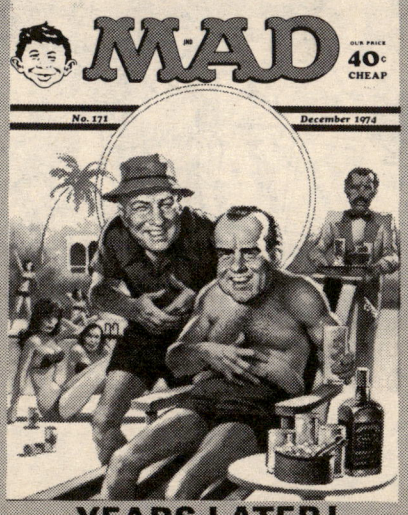

YEARS LATER!

SERGIO ARAGONES DEPT.
A MAD LOOK

AT "STAR WARS"

ARTIST & WRITER: SERGIO ARAGONES

WASTE MEASUREMENTS DEPT.

HOW COME YOU WORRY ABOUT...

WHEN....

ARTIST: JACK RICKARD
WRITER: STAN HART

HOW COME YOU WORRY ABOUT...

...unemployment, the recession, the state of our union and the world...

WHEN...

...you never even bothered to vote in the last three Presidential elections!

... whether the right person will inherit Howard Hughes's fortune ...

... you can't even raise enough cash to keep up the car payments!

HOW COME YOU WORRY ABOUT...

... if Princess Margaret is lonely and miserable since her separation from Anthony Armstrong Jones ...

WHEN...

... you sit by yourself in your room all day watching the flies make love!

...who'll win the Academy Awards...

...you can't even afford to go to see the overpriced movies the actors in contention are getting rich on!

...whether Barbara Walters is happy at ABC with her 5 million dollar contract...

...you're working in some grimy sweatshop for the minimum wage.

HOW COME YOU WORRY ABOUT...

...what's happening to Chris Evert and Jimmy Connors' relationship...

WHEN...

...that bum you call your boyfriend hasn't called you in over a week now!

...whether Tom Seaver will be getting $100,000 or $175,000 this year...

...you've been killing yourself trying to get a five buck raise at work!

HOW COME YOU WORRY ABOUT...

... Joe Morgan's future whenever his batting average falls below .310 ...

WHEN...

... you've fallen below "C" in half your subjects, and "D" in the rest!

HOW COME YOU WORRY ABOUT...

... whether Jackie Gleason can make a successful comeback ...

WHEN...

... you can't even get yourself a job because you're over 45!

HOW COME YOU WORRY ABOUT...

...if Richard Nixon is a happy man in his virtual exile at San Clemente...

WHEN...

...you're stuck in a lousy apartment, and you never even committed a crime!

HOW COME YOU WORRY ABOUT...

. . . who's going to make this year's
"Ten Best Dressed Women" list . . .

. . . you've got to buy your clothes
in "schlock" stores . . . or go naked!

HOW COME YOU WORRY ABOUT...

...whether Joan and Ted Kennedy's marriage is really a happy one...

WHEN...

...the last happy moment you had with your crummy Husband was when he paused before saying, "I do!"

ON THE JOB, STRAINING DEPT.

There's a "Baseball Hall of Fame" and a "Football Hall of Fame" and a "Basketball Hall of Fame" and a "Hockey Hall of Fame." There's an "Aviation Hall of Fame" and a "Great Americans Hall of Fame." But what about the everyday slobs that have to work from 9 to 5 in offices all across America? Why not honor their great feats in . . .

THE OFFICE WORKERS' HALL OF FAME

ARTIST: BOB CLARKE

WRITER: DICK DE BARTOLO

JULIET WYBRANTS
LEGAL SECRETARY
SUDEM, SERVEM & SETTLE
JANUARY 1976 TO DECEMBER 1976

HOLDS THE WORLD'S RECORD FOR
"OFFICE WORKER HONESTY" BY
LEAVING HER PLACE OF EMPLOYMENT
EVERY EVENING FOR A SOLID YEAR
WITHOUT TAKING HOME ANY SUPPLIES!

RAY PICHON
LOAN ARRANGER
TONTO FINANCE CORPORATION
FRIDAY, APRIL 8, 1977

ON THE ABOVE DATE, RAY PICHON TOOK THE DAY
OFF FOR RELIGIOUS OBSERVANCE, AND THEN
ACTUALLY WENT TO A HOUSE OF WORSHIP!

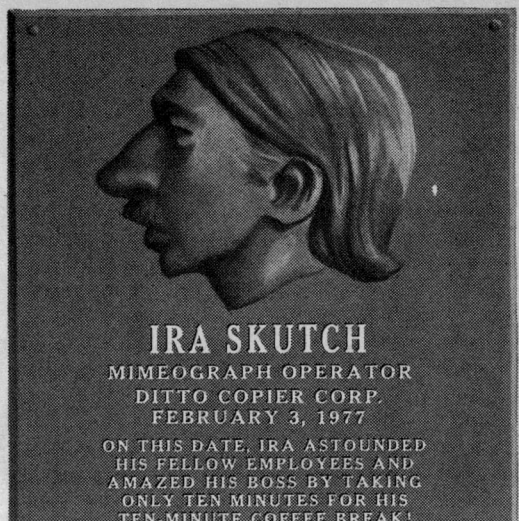

IRA SKUTCH
MIMEOGRAPH OPERATOR
DITTO COPIER CORP.
FEBRUARY 3, 1977

ON THIS DATE, IRA ASTOUNDED
HIS FELLOW EMPLOYEES AND
AMAZED HIS BOSS BY TAKING
ONLY TEN MINUTES FOR HIS
TEN-MINUTE COFFEE BREAK!

BRUNO ZIRATO
ORDER CLERK
NEW DEHLI DELI PRODUCTS, INC.
FEBRUARY, 1976

THIS PLAQUE HONORS BRUNO ZIRATO
WHO, DURING THE ENTIRE MONTH
CITED ABOVE, NEVER MADE MORE
THAN ONE PERSONAL PHONE CALL
IN ANY GIVEN EIGHT HOUR SHIFT!

ROBERT NORDSKOG

ASSISTANT EXECUTIVE
AMALGAMATED
RUST CORP., INC.
OCTOBER 19, 1976

ON THIS DATE, ROBERT
NORDSKOG TOOK A
PROSPECTIVE CLIENT TO
DINNER AT HIS COMPANY'S
EXPENSE, AND HE DID NOT
ORDER THE MOST EXPENSIVE
ITEM ON THE MENU!
FURTHERMORE, HE ONLY
HAD ONE DRINK,
AND HE SKIPPED DESSERT!

JAY WOLPERT
ARCHITECT
TILT & SINK BUILDING CORP.
JUNE 2, 1976

ON THE ABOVE DATE, JAY WOLPERT
ASKED HIS FINELY PROPORTIONED
SECRETARY, WHOSE DIMENSIONS ARE
38-23-36, TO STAY AFTER FIVE SO
THEY COULD "WORK LATE"...AND
THEN THEY DID IN FACT WORK LATE!

ELLIOTT FELDMAN
MAIL ORDER CLERK
SCHLOCK PRODUCTS, CORP.
NOVEMBER 3, 1976

ON THE ABOVE DATE, ELLIOTT PUT A PERSONAL LETTER THROUGH THE POSTAGE MACHINE, AND THEN PAID PETTY CASH 13¢ FOR THE STAMP!

DIANE JANEVER
SECRETARY-TYPIST

HUNT AND PECK PRODUCTS CORP.
AUGUST 10, 1976

ON THE ABOVE DATE DIANE JANEVER ALLOWED HER BOSS TO GIVE HER A LETTER TO TYPE WITHOUT SWEARING AT HIM UNDER HER BREATH... EVEN THOUGH IT WAS FIVE MINUTES TO QUITTING TIME!

HOWARD FELSHER

UNEMPLOYED OFFICE WORKER
JANUARY
FEBRUARY & MARCH, 1977

DURING THE MONTHS INDICATED, HE COLLECTED UNEMPLOYMENT BENEFITS. BUT AT THE SAME TIME, HE WAS ACTUALLY LOOKING FOR WORK, AND HE REALLY DID HAVE JOB INTERVIEWS WITH ALL OF THE PEOPLE HE'D LISTED ON HIS UNEMPLOYMENT QUESTIONNAIRES!

ROBERT SHERMAN

SHOE SALESMAN
FOOT FETISH
FITTERS, INC.
FRIDAY, MARCH 11, 1977

ON THIS DATE, ROBERT DISTINGUISHED HIMSELF BY FILING AN EXPENSE ACCOUNT FOR THE EXACT AMOUNT OF HIS EXPENSES!

PHILLIP WAYNE

STOCK CLERK & GOFER
BULL, BEAR & BUST, BROKERS

EVERY MONDAY DURING SEPTEMBER
OCTOBER AND NOVEMBER, 1977

FOR HIS OUTSTANDING RESTRAINT,
THIS PLAQUE IS PRESENTED TO THE
ABOVE NAMED INDIVIDUAL FOR NEVER
HAVING MENTIONED ONE WORD ABOUT
WEEK-END FOOTBALL DURING NORMAL
BUSINESS HOURS

MIMI O'BRIEN

CLERK-TYPIST-RECEPTIONIST
LOW PAYING INDUSTRIES, INC.
FRIDAY, DECEMBER 24, 1976

ON THIS DATE, MIMI O'BRIEN, WHO
WAS RECEIVING THE MINIMUM WAGE,
CALLED THE ACCOUNTING DEPARTMENT
TO INFORM THEM THAT SOMEONE HAD
ACCIDENTALLY OVERPAID HER $10

UP THEIRS! DEPT.

ARTIST: BOB JONES
WRITER: LARRY SIEGEL
IDEA BY: MARC BILGREY

YOU DON'T GIVE A %#*&!*? WHAT OTHER PEOPLE THINK WHEN...

... you show up at the ridiculous hour of 8:30 P.M., even though the party invitation clearly states you are *expected* at 8:30 P.M.

... you wear T-shirts that don't have idiotic slogans or pictures on them.

... you date a Stewardess ... and admit to your friends the next day that you didn't make out.

... you're a Producer and you make a movie that takes place *after* 1947.

. . . you take a trip to Hollywood and you don't stop once to take pictures in front of Lucille Ball's house (or ring her bell and ask for an autographed picture for your Aunt).

. . . you have crooked teeth, and you refuse to have braces put on them.

. . . you give your new baby a good old-fashioned ethnic name like Moe or Izzy or Pasquale, instead of today's usual crop like Lance or Ian or Craig or Charlemagne.

. . . you buy yourself a pet *dog* instead of a pet ocelot, or pet monkey, or pet snake or pet rock.

... you own a car without a bumper sticker.

... you have a freshly-paved sidewalk in front of your house with no initials scratched in it.

... you hire a *White* player for your Pro Basketball Team.

... you buy a fantastically revealing swim suit ... and actually *swim* in it.

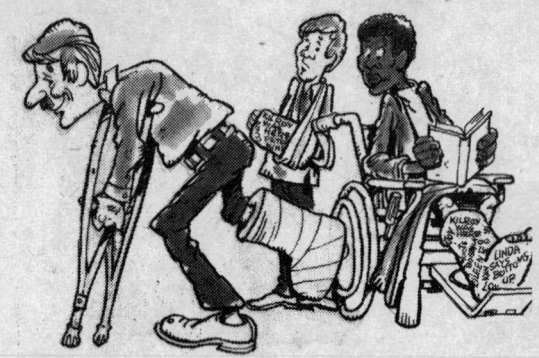

. . . you hobble around on a broken leg in a cast with no funny messages by your friends written all over it.

. . . you admit to the Newsdealer you buy MAD for yourself . . . and not for some fictitious 12-year-old idiot nephew.

DON MARTIN DEPT.

ONE AFTERNOON IN ACUPULCO

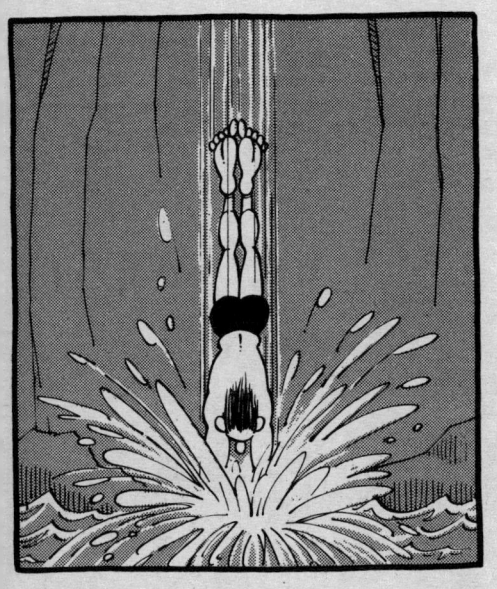

HERE WE GO WITH MAD'S VERSION OF THE POPULAR TV

We built a "Moronic Man"! It's the very same technology to build a "Moronic WOMAN"...!!

I must get rid of this terrible habit of saving money by buying "Seconds"... especially when it comes to something important... like a PARACHUTE! H-E-L-L-P!!

Well, Jammy, it's 400 operations and 2 Band-Aids later! How do you feel Jammy? Are you alright Jammy, say something!! Doctor! What's wrong?!? We spent six million dollars on her ... and she can't even talk!!!

Batteries are extra! Don't you read the fine print?! Batteries are always extra!

Er... well... it's ALMOST the same technology to build a "Moronic Woman"!!

SHOW THAT OPENS EACH WEEK LIKE THIS:

TRAN-SISTER DEPT.

The MORONIC WOMAN

ARTIST: MORT DRUCKER WRITER: DICK DE BARTOLO

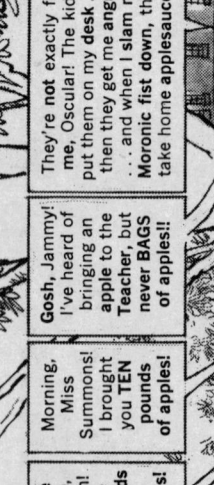

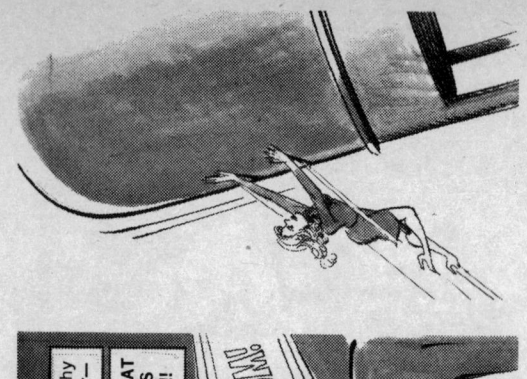

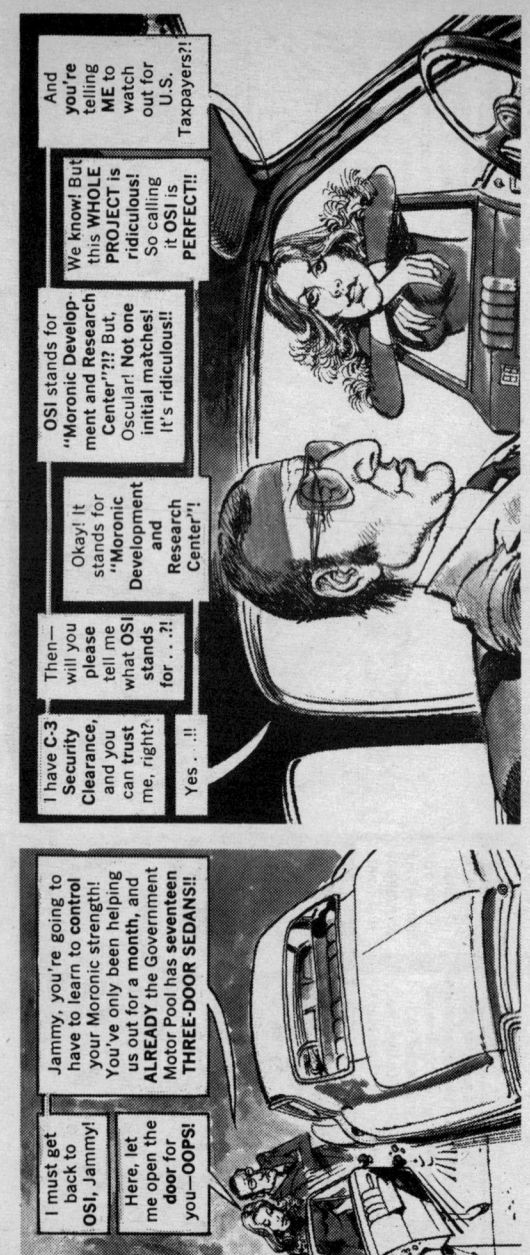

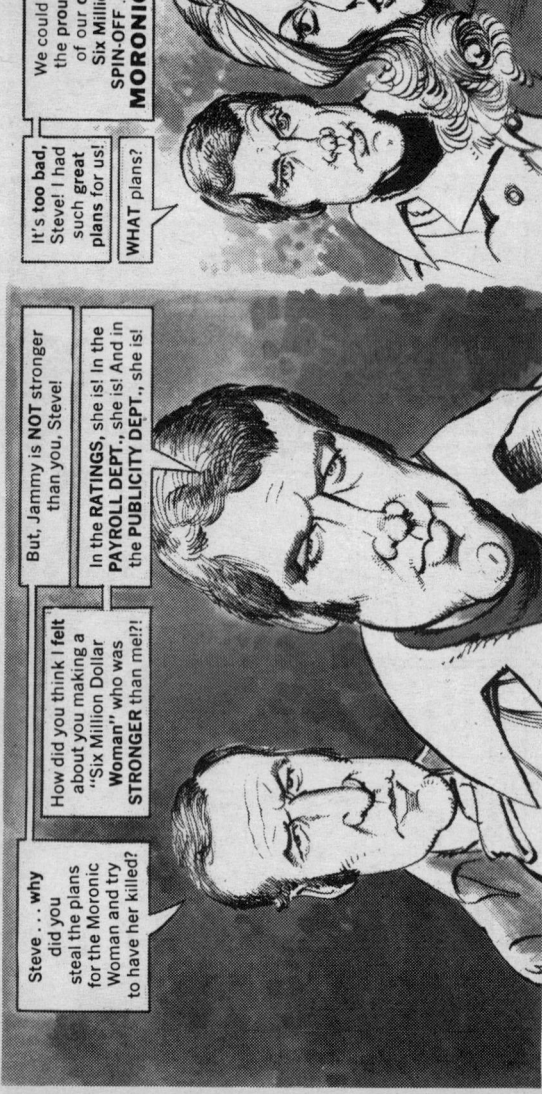